Barry Fantoni, novelist, broadcaster, jazz musician, reviewer, illustrator, film and TV actor, *Private Eye* contributor, *The Times* diary cartoonist, was born on February 28, 1940.

Barry Fantoni's Chinese Horoscopes

THE MONKEY

SPHERE BOOKS LIMITED

SPHERE BOOKS LIMITED

Penguin Books Ltd, 27 Wrights Lane, London W8 5TZ (Publishing and Editorial)
and Harmondsworth, Middlesex, England (Distribution and Warehouse)
Viking Penguin Inc., 40 West 23rd Street, New York, New York 10010, USA
Penguin Books Australia Ltd, Ringwood, Victoria, Australia
Penguin Books Canada Ltd, 2801 John Street, Markham, Ontario, Canada L3R 1B4
Penguin Books (NZ) Ltd, 182–190 Wairau Road, Auckland 10, New Zealand

First published in Great Britain by Sphere Books Ltd 1987

Copyright © 1987 by Barry Fantoni

Made and printed in Great Britain by
Richard Clay Ltd, Bungay, Suffolk
Filmset in 9½/10pt Photina

To my family of Roosters

Acknowledgements

I should like to express my thanks to all those many friends, relatives and strangers who have both knowingly and otherwise helped with the compilation of this book. I should like to thank in particular Gillian Jason who researched the beautiful Chinese illustrations, The British Library for granting permission to reproduce them, and Dr Hin Hung Ho for the delightful calligraphy. But the bulk of my gratitude is reserved for my Rooster wife who ploughed on relentlessly with the list of celebrities whose names are scattered throughout, and without which this book could never have been written.

Introduction

How do you introduce yourself? Do you first give your name, or say what school you went to, or where you live, or what kind of job you do? Whatever you say, the chances are that you will be attempting in some small way to summarise who you imagine yourself to be, and hoping that the label you choose will do the *real* you justice.

In the East, however, introductions may take on a very different form. Because of a system that has evolved throughout Eastern civilisation, everyone has a birth sign named after one of the twelve animals that make up the Chinese Horoscope. Consequently, when two strangers meet, instead of giving their names, they might well refer to their animal sign. 'I am a Monkey,' one might say.

'Pleased to meet you,' might come the reply, 'I am a Dragon.'

As a result of this simple greeting, a great deal of unspoken information will have changed hands. In that particular case, if they had met to discuss business, both Monkey and Dragon will probably have parted on good terms. However, if the Dragon had been a Buffalo I suspect that the two Chinese businessmen would have given the meeting a miss. And for a very good reason. For the Peoples of the East, an individual's personal animal sign, dictated by the year of birth, plays a central role in the conduct of their daily lives. Since I was introduced to the system some thirteen years ago, it has revolutionised mine. Chinese horoscopes have shown me a completely fresh way of viewing human behaviour, one that can be of great practical use. It can, for example, guide us to the best business associate, help us in our choice of marriage partners and even suggest the ideal lover. Chinese Horoscopes tell us why we dress like we do, why some of us save every penny while others spend without caring. We learn why some are content to sit at home while others travel to the four corners of the globe. It explains who we really are, not only to the world at large, but more importantly to ourselves.

No one is certain how the Chinese Horoscope first came into being, but there is, as with all mysteries, a legend which I believe makes up in poetical charm what it lacks in scientific probability.

Five centuries before the birth of Christ, so the legend has it, the Buddha sent out an invitation to all the animals in his Kingdom, asking if they would join him in the New Year celebrations. For reasons that seem only known to the animals themselves, only twelve turned up. In order of arrival there came: the rat, the buffalo, the tiger, the cat, the dragon, the snake, the horse, the goat, the monkey, the rooster, the dog and last of all the pig. Cheered by their presence, the Buddha decided to show his gratitude by honouring each animal with a year, calling it by their name. Moreover, all people born in that year would inherit the animal's characteristics. Monkeys would be wise and clever, Dogs would be anxious and loyal. Unlike Western astrology which is based on the movement of the sun and the stars, the Chinese use the lunar cycle. There are twelve moons in a lunar cycle, plus an extra moon every thirteen (our Blue Moon), which is why the Chinese New Year never falls on the same day. So, with twelve moons and twelve animals there evolved a perfect pattern. Heaven alone knows what would have happened if a few camels and ducks had decided to show up for the Buddha's party!

Given such an explanation, the most obvious question for us Western sceptics to ask is how on earth can all those born in the same year inherit the same characteristics? The answer is of course that we are not all identical. And it was only when I had stopped asking that same question about the thousands of people I didn't know, asking instead if it were true of myself, that I discovered that the system of Chinese Horoscopes really worked. Testing the system first on my own sign, then on my family and friends, and finally on a large number of celebrities whose lives I am familiar with, I was left in no doubt that it was startlingly accurate. In other words, instead of generalising, I looked at specific cases. And once I had shed my scepticism I began to understand more clearly the Chinese view of the twelve animal signs, and the influence they exercise over our lives.

The sign of our parents, the sign of marriage and business partners and the signs of our children all create variations on the way our own animal sign influences us. The eager to please Dragon son will benefit enormously from his adoring Rooster mother, while the passionate Rat will find the anxious Dog impervious to her advances. Time of birth is another factor which determines a subtle difference in temperament. Goats born in the summer will be less capricious than those born in winter, whereas Snakes born during a sudden thunderstorm will be in danger all their lives.

This book gives an idea of the markedly different attitudes between the two cultures of East and West. To seek pleasure and enjoyment from life is an inherent part of Chinese philosophy. The West on the other hand, frowns on those who treat life like a game. The East recognises that the games we play, both as adults and children, are a form of make-believe which not only enhances life but in some mysterious way offers us the key to true self-discovery. The West puts men on the Moon, the East puts men in touch with their real selves; or in other words, the animal within.

Clearly no one can foretell our destiny, and even if one could, so many conflicting factors would make escaping it an absolute impossibility. The Chinese Horoscope has little or nothing to do with the Western signs of the Zodiac. What it teaches is not a plan for tomorrow, but a way to know yourself today and every day. To learn who we are through our influencing animal is to take part in a wonderful ancient game that will make our lives both richer and happier.

Barry Fantoni's
Chinese Horoscopes

THE MONKEY

猴

1908	February 2nd to January 21st	1909
1920	February 20th to February 7th	1921
1932	February 6th to January 25th	1933
1944	January 25th to February 12th	1945
1956	February 12th to January 30th	1957
1968	January 30th to February 16th	1969
1980	February 16th to February 4th	1981
1992	February 4th to January 22nd	1993

Some Monkey's queer grimaces.
Forestalling human faces,
Fill the gaps and spaces
That link two ancient races.

Leon Underwood

The Year of the Monkey

If you regard yourself as a wilting flower, then the hyperactive year of the Monkey is definitely not for you. Everything is up for grabs, and it's a case of first come first served. And if there's to be a rule, it will, I am afraid, be the rule of anarchy. Under the influence of the mischievous Monkey, anything can happen, and almost certainly will. You will wake up each morning and read the newspaper headlines with growing disbelief. In 1920, Americans woke up to find prohibition had been introduced, and in 1968 slumbering Parisians opened their bleary eyes to find the streets full of rioting students – the most serious of its kind since the last century.

The accent everywhere will be on trend, on posture, on novelty: Monkeys love fun. But in spite of its superficiality, the Monkey year will give birth to a great many discoveries and there will be great strides made in the fields of science and technology. It's a time for new ideas, new methods, new worlds. Britain's first atomic power station was opened in 1956, and in the same year the House of Commons rejected a motion to retain the death penalty.

The year of the Monkey is not one in which to sit around and contemplate your navel, not unless that's the current trend. The secret is to take chances, to take risks, to deal and double-deal. In 1968 there was an almost unprecedented rush on gold, and at one point the Stock Exchange closed down. In 1980 Lord Thomson put *The Times* and *The Sunday Times* up for sale.

One way or another, political issues will be settled. The Hungarian uprising was finally squashed by Soviet troops in 1956 and later that year Pakistan proclaimed itself an Islamic republic. Nothing that happens in the year of the Monkey will be pint-sized or insignificant. Senator Robert Kennedy and the Reverend Martin Luther King were both assassinated in 1968, and in 1980, John Lennon was gunned down outside his New York apartment.

The trick to learn in the year of the Monkey is not to run against the tide. It is not a time for moralists or stick-in-the-muds. In 1968 the Pope issued his encyclical banning of all methods of artificial birth control, and found it met with a largely hostile reception. Evangelists should talk less to their flock, and more to their tax lawyers. But the world of popular entertainment will flourish, and there will be many new stars in the galaxy of sport, music and cinema. The very first public broadcasting station was opened by the Marconi Company in 1920. The greatest popular entertainer of all time made his disc debut in 1956: 'Heartbreak Hotel' was the title of the record that was to introduce Elvis Presley to a public who continue to buy his albums in millions.

The Monkey's year will begin and end in a restless pursuit of fun and profit. But if things don't work out, don't expect to hang around and mope. The Monkey just swings skilfully, effortlessly, onto the next branch. And do not expect the Big Love Affair to last a lifetime. Those who are lucky at cards are often, so it is said, unlucky in love. There'll be plenty of five card poker in the year of the Monkey, but the luck will, I'm afraid, run out at the bedroom door.

Monkeys are born under the sign of fantasy

The Monkey Personality

---

*'Roll the dice and throw a six.
Enter the wise and clever Monkey'*

It is an inescapable fact that of all the animals, the Monkey bears the strongest resemblance to Mankind. Whether you accept Darwin's theory of evolution, or throw your lot in with the Bible thumping fundamentalists, there can be little doubt that when we come face to face with a Monkey, we in some senses see ourselves. And once we have examined those born under the sign of the Monkey we will discover a sobering truth; Monkeys are blessed not only with the very best Man has to offer, but also, sadly, his worst.

On the credit side, the Monkey has great wisdom. He has a high regard for knowledge and has an extraordinary power to reason out the most complex of problems, seemingly with no effort. He knows the rewards that this world has to offer, and that wealth and power are the means to achieve them. Not one to pick up the sword to attain his goals, the Monkey instead uses his logic, his wit, and his intuition, which seems to tell him the precise time to act. Utterly charming, resourceful, with an overwhelming conceit that we invariably forgive, the Monkey will go as far as it is possible in whatever field he chooses. And if the Monkey has a foundation stone on which all his enterprises are built, it will be engraved with the two words: *Wit* and *Wisdom*. If you were born in the year of the Monkey, you share your sign with: Leonardo da Vinci, Liz Taylor, Sir Christopher Wren, the great escapologist Harry Houdini, Bette Davis, Peter O'Toole, Charles

Dickens, Ronald Searle, Diana Ross, Rod Stewart and Koo Stark.

The Monkey also has a wonderful gift for figures and you'll find his mathematical genius popping up in areas as distinct from each other as commerce, science, architecture and music – you need a cool head when counting the beats to a bar. But of all his qualities, the Monkey's closest link with Man is to be found in his sense of humour. His wit is not caustic or blunt, bawdy or cynical. What it does is bubble with a mixture of very gentle rib tickling and the purest wit. At its best, the Monkey's wit resembles the subtle sayings of Eastern sages. You can quite easily picture the wise old Monkey sitting under the shade of a Lotus tree, surrounded by enchanted admirers, and hear him telling the assembly, 'He who plants a forest in the morning cannot expect to saw planks in the evening.' Or, 'Those without shoes should think of those without feet.'

Bearing in mind these ancient proverbs, it is not surprising to learn that the Buddha himself was a Monkey.

But if the irresistible Monkey mirrors all our finest qualities, how far does he go in aping those we respect least? Certainly you will look long and hard for any deeply felt scruples, and you might as well find the proverbial needle in a haystack as discover a Monkey with a strong ethical code. It is just not part of his make-up. Crafty, shy, sly, artful, these are the words used in describing the Monkey's inferior side. Sharp practice is very often the Monkey's stock in trade, and success his only goal. And if the Monkey has a tool it is deception, which he uses as mechanics use a universal spanner.

However, it must be said that the Monkey has such guile, such a highly developed sense of his own superiority that he is very often unable to distinguish fact from fiction. He will, on many occasions, believe his fabrications to be the real thing. After all, the Monkey is born under the sign of fantasy.

Arrogant, and having little or no respect for the opinions of others, the Monkey will often get clean away with his tricks. And strangers are easily taken in by the Monkey's fast talk. Only those who live close to the Monkey know how to catch him. In this respect, the bushmen of the Kalahari desert in Southern Africa have got the Monkey's number, tricking him in true Monkey style. They do it simply by relying on the Monkey's greed. First the bushman digs a tunnel in a mound of earth roughly the length of a Monkey's arm, and at the end of it, he makes a slightly larger hole. After making sure that the tunnel is only wide enough for a Monkey to place an open hand through, the bushman deposits a pile of sugar in the hollow. When the Monkey puts his arm in and grabs the sugar, his fist naturally has to shut. But with his fist closed around the sugar, it is too large to pull out through the tunnel. Rather than let his prize go, the Monkey foolishly, avariciously, holds on. Even when the bushman appears, the Monkey will never let go. That sugar is his! Poor, misguided Monkey. So the lesson is quite clear when dealing with a Monkey: don't try to win an open confrontation, he is the world's number one smart alec. A war of words will get you nowhere. Just offer him some sweet wine and a huge helping of chocolate fudge cake, and wait till he's too drunk or fat to fight.

The combination of a sharp mind, opportunism and thrift provides the Monkey with all he needs to become a candidate for the super tax league. Indeed, the Monkey may pile up treasures for himself, and do so with the kind of panache that will always hit the headlines. And Monkeys seldom specialise, preferring always to diversify their talents as much as possible. They might make their first million late in life, like the famous American primitive painter, Grandma Moses, or before they leave their teens – remember Bjorn Borg?

Fundamental to the Monkey's prosperity, and equally essential to his great social adaptability, is his quite extraordinary memory. Buffaloes, Dogs, Pigs and Snakes can all be relied on to dredge up some half forgotten fact at the drop of a hat, but no other animal can lay claim to having such a remarkable gift as the Monkey's memory. And it is perhaps no accident. The Monkey, for all his quick wit and craft, is usually insecure at heart. He needs to be shown love openly and craves attention. It is here that a good memory is not just a blessing, but an essential piece of equipment. After all, if he can immediately remember your name, little details about your likes and dislikes, facts about your private life and so on, he is well on the way to winning you over. How fascinating you must be for the Monkey – such a charming creature – to have taken so much trouble to have remembered all that about you; *you* of all people! But flattering you by remembering the name of your eldest son, the school he goes to and how high he came in his mock GCEs is all part of the Monkey's bag of tricks. It is, in effect, a confidence trick in the fullest sense. The truth is that the Monkey's memory is second nature, and moreover, he is the same warm hearted, smiling, laughing, fun loving, fun person with every single person he meets. No matter who it is: taxi driver or oldest friend, stranger or relative – all are one to the Monkey in search of security. Never one to be weighed down with compassion, the Monkey's motto might easily be that of con men everywhere, 'here come the mugs'.

An outstanding memory is of course essential if you want to become a linguist. The present Pope, John Paul II is a Monkey, and I understand he speaks six languages more or less perfectly. Fred Housego, the taxi driver winner of *Mastermind* is a Monkey, and so was the original Memory Man, Leslie Welch.

Allied to the Monkey's astonishing power of recall is his avid thirst for knowledge. No matter whether it is a piece of junk mail that has just fallen on the doormat, or the latest Pulitzer Prize novel, the Monkey will read it avidly, and very often without a hint of judgement. For the Monkey, knowledge is simply knowledge, to be stored away for use on a future occasion. Moral issues are not his concern in this respect. And his appetite for new experiences will lead a Monkey to try anything once. Just watch the Monkey at the table, dipping his finger into everyone else's pie. If it is new, if he's never had it before, you can count on the Monkey to be in the front of the queue of those wanting to try a sample. And the Monkey won't stop at your summer pudding. So watch out if he takes a fancy to your wife (or husband).

In commerce, the arts and sciences, the Monkey's combination of a retentive and attentive mind, plus his never ending quest for new experiences, makes him a formidable opponent. But in spite of his remarkable memory and thirst for knowledge, the Monkey is seldom an originator. Just think of those crowds in front of the Monkey cage at the zoo. They stand there pulling faces and before you know it, the Monkey is doing the exact same thing. All the tricks the chimp learns for his comic tea party he learned from us. Of course, there are exceptions. The first painter ever to cover his canvas with coloured squares, Piet Mondrian, was a Monkey. So too, was the greatest original in all jazz, the alto saxophonist, Charlie Parker. He revolutionised jazz in the forties and influenced millions of musicians. Yet Charlie Parker always claimed his highly original style was modelled on a long forgotten player whom he'd heard as a young man in his home town of Kansas City. And how original is Roy Hattersley, or Shirley Conran? Like rag and bone men, Monkeys take a little from here, a bit from there and often without the faintest idea that they are doing it, sell the goods off as their own. I remember telling my young Monkey sister-in-law an idea I had to throw a swanky dinner party, complete with waiters, buckets of champagne, and guests in full evening dress. But it would all take place in a rented bedsit in the most dreadful area of Earls Court, and when the silver lids would be lifted, all my guests would find to assuage their appetites would be piles of bangers and mash. Some time later I heard the same idea told back to me by her aunt, who in turn had been told it by my sister-in-law, who had apparently given the impression she had just thought of it.

Put without frills, what the Monkey tends to offer is frequently a touch superficial. But however skin deep his knowledge is it is nevertheless extremely broad. And his stories, whatever their source, always hold our attention. No one tells a tale better than a Monkey, or laces it with such charm and wit. And it must be emphasised that the Monkey has a terrific sense of humour, one that gets him both into and out of his fair share of scrapes. Whatever else, there will be no shortage of near misses and close calls in the fast and furious life of the Monkey.

Once the Monkey has decided on a course of action, he must act at once. If a Monkey is kept waiting, he'll quickly move on to something else – and there are always plenty of options, he makes sure of that. I knew a Monkey who planned to go to the United States, but got fed up with waiting around for her visa and went to Israel instead. She came back to England and applied to go to art school, but she'd left it too late to do any work for her portfolio and got turned down. She then went back to Sussex University (where she had planned her American trip), thought about becoming a flying doctor, applied for an American visa . . . The one thing you can say about a Monkey who stares defeat in the face is he'll admit to it. There'll be no false heroics. This has the advantage, of course, of conserving the Monkey's energy, and gives him time to prepare to strike again.

Because Monkeys must experience everything, and given the chance, all at once, they adore travelling. The open road holds up the endless promise of ever new and increasingly wonderful adventures. This is particularly true of young Monkeys, who dominate the autoroutes of the world with their hitched thumbs and engaging smiles.

But if it seems that Monkeys have more going for them than most, that too is perhaps a result of the Monkey's cunning. For all his artfulness and acumen, the Monkey finds little joy if he or she falls in love. For many, the heart poses no end of threats, but not for the Monkey. If anything, Monkeys treat love far too lightly, seeing it as just another game in which they hold all the aces. But love is not like a game of poker. No matter whether it is a life-long commitment or a casual affair, there can be no winners or losers in love. What is needed is a mutual respect and the constant necessity to share – the two qualities that the Monkey has in short supply. Try as he or she might to settle down, the ever present need to try out new experiences will exert itself. No one will ever fully satisfy him, because the Monkey never really wants satisfaction. A tendency towards casual affairs may sometimes lead lady Monkeys off the straight and narrow, and if they are not extremely careful, onto the streets. And I know several lady Monkeys who have absolutely no regrets at having become high-class mistresses.

For all his excesses, and acquisitiveness, the Monkey is capable of great charity. He will genuinely rejoice in your successes as well as commiserate in your failures. And when the Monkey calls, he will never come empty-handed. Even if it is no more than a valueless trinket, there'll always be a little gift especially for you. And when you find a postcard on your doormat from some far flung corner of the globe, it will be a Monkey who was wishing *you* were there. How the Monkey loves to please. How considerate.

Monkey ladies often have fair and sensitive skin. Their faces redden easily and they tend to suffer minor skin complaints. They dress almost entirely to impress, and spend a lot of time on their very beautiful hair (they would like you to believe that it grows so beautifully naturally). But although they dress to knock you dead, they do it with taste. Indeed, in the years when the world of fashion talked about the best dressed woman, the Duchess of Windsor, a Monkey if ever there was one, held the title for fifteen years on the trot.

The Monkey male is neat and dresses without much interest in trendy fashions. His work room will be functional and even sparse, resembling in some cases, a monk's cell. But if two Monkeys get together, the Monkey mansion will end up a shambles. But whatever the state of the living room, two Monkeys make a splendid marriage, and are high on the list of all time great combinations. However, Monkeys will not be heartbroken if Mr Right never comes along. I know a Monkey lady who has four different children from four separate relationships – two lawful husbands and two live-in hubbies. She could charm rain to fall on the Sahara, that one!

Whatever the Monkey chooses as his first profession, it will in all likelihood not be the one for which he becomes famous. Former world champion snooker player, Ray Reardon, was a miner and a policeman before becoming a household name in the snooker field. And the painter Paul Gauguin was a bank clerk before he packed up his paints and set sail for the South Seas. Monkeys change their husbands and wives almost as often as they change jobs. Ethel Merman was married four times, and Rex Harrison has been married to six different women. But should a Monkey stick to a job, he would be well advised to choose a post in which he can employ his agile mind, power to organise and phenomenal memory. Monkey ladies make exceptional personal secretaries. Often they exert more influence than their boss, carving out a small autonomy within the framework of their organisation. In this position they can exercise the maximum control with the minimum of responsibility. The boss will carry the can for the bad deals as well as take credit for the good. But that won't bother the Monkey, who will herself know the real power behind the throne. And as a dealer in sharp practice, the Monkey has no rival. 'Softly, softly, catchee Monkey', is one saying. 'Softly, softly, clinchee deal', is another.

The Chinese say that of all the animals the Monkey is the best suited for the rigours of travel. It is believed that Monkeys are capable of adapting to any situation and can turn even the worst plights round to their advantage. Because Monkeys have the great gift of mimicry, they can pick up foreign languages in no time at all. No matter where they are it is seldom long before you discover the Monkey deep in conversation with the local fishermen, discussing prevailing winds in their own tongue. Monkeys have an unquenchable thirst for knowledge and will try anything once. This adds up to a holiday well off the beaten track. Never ones to throw their money away in a hurry, price might well determine the Monkey's destination – good value is what is called for. A canoe trip up the Amazon is one suggestion.

The three phases of a Monkey's life will be marked by an unsettled childhood, with his youthful blend of artfulness and sense of superiority constantly placing him on the wrong side of authority. But his brushes with power will toughen him up for the middle period of his life in which he'll be on the receiving end of some pretty hard knocks. He'll make a name for himself, no doubt, but his home life will never be as stable as it might and there will be many out to play him at his own game. Old age will be kinder to the Monkey, but the thirst for knowledge and new experiences will never leave him, no matter what age he lives to. I have a suspicion that those old age pensioners photographed holding university degrees are all born in the year of the Monkey. But the Chinese warn that all Monkeys are in danger of dying a sudden death a long way from home. Monkey, be warned!

*Monkeys are careful with money,
but they always make plenty*

Monkey as Parent

The Monkey will often become a fine parent, presenting his children with one of the most important of all tools – an inquiring mind. A child under the roof of a Monkey will never lack stimulation, and will be given every encouragement to learn whatever he desires. And there will be no shortage of affection and love that comes direct from the heart. Even if the Monkey parent gets divorced, the children will always come first, no matter what. The baby Rat, especially a boy, will get all he asks from his mother Monkey, and will seize every opportunity that's offered him with both hands. The young Pig will also flourish against the Monkey's warmth and intelligence. And a Cat child will never be bored. With so much clever conversation to keep her mind occupied the Kitten will not be so easily frightened by every door that's slammed shut by a gust of wind. And Daddy Monkey will be so proud of his Cat daughter's artistic achievements. He'll also delight in the talents of his daughter Goat, but won't be so thrilled when the young lady starts to play him at his own tricks.

The Horse daughter will have no time for a Monkey mother who spends all her time in front of the mirror, more so since that's where the baby Mare wants to be. But at least they'll be able to swop clothes. Vanity, however, is not the problem facing the Buffalo in the Monkey parent's home. He is not over-enthusiastic about his father Monkey's less than modest ways, and wonders where is the substance to what he is being told? But if nothing else, the Buffalo infant will be loved, probably because he *is* so critical. Monkeys like any kind of lively mind, but the young Rooster will expect high standards from her Monkey parent; nothing the Monkey can do or say will sway her to an easier manner. Jokes are fine in their place, but the Monkey father really oughtn't to laugh at his Rooster daughter's upright opinions quite so openly! There'll be no laughter at the baby Tiger, whose vigour and daring will win approval all round, though the Tiger must learn when not to interrupt her Monkey mother when she's on the phone. The Monkey father might find his Snake son a little silent, even withdrawn, but he'll forgive this trait in his Snake daughter – she is so lovely, so bewitching . . . even the Monkey is enchanted. There isn't a Dragon son born who doesn't expect his parent to be fascinated by his every word. And with the Monkey as a parent he'll have a captive and doting audience. But is it really healthy for the darling Dragon to be showered with Oscars at such an early age? He could grow up to become a monster.

Unfortunately for the puppy Dog, there'll be plenty of criticism coming his way. Too much, usually. He can find no

Compatibility of Monkey Parent and Child

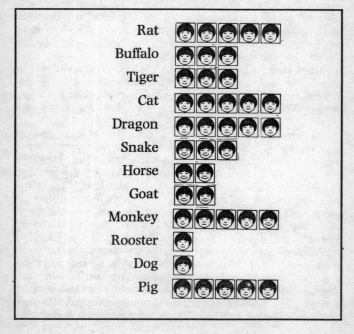

Rat	🐵🐵🐵🐵🐵
Buffalo	🐵🐵🐵
Tiger	🐵🐵🐵
Cat	🐵🐵🐵🐵🐵🐵
Dragon	🐵🐵🐵🐵🐵
Snake	🐵🐵🐵
Horse	🐵🐵
Goat	🐵
Monkey	🐵🐵🐵🐵🐵
Rooster	🐵
Dog	🐵
Pig	🐵🐵🐵🐵🐵

substance in his father's advice, no calls to a more perfect world. Dog children want ideals from their Monkey dad, not six ways to win at cards. Baby Monkeys, conversely, want nothing else from their Monkey parent. No wonder Monkeys are so full of tricks.

Monkeys are acquisitive and have wonderful memories

Monkey in Business

There can be no doubting the Monkey's great ability to make money, and make the most of himself while doing it. For as much as the Monkey enjoys having a stable bank balance, he enjoys doing it in style almost as much. Better working as an individual, the Monkey nevertheless pairs up well with the assertive and flashy Dragon. Both love the big time and will give each other a leg up as they climb the social and financial mountains. If the lady is a Monkey she will make an excellent personal assistant to a Dragon boss. And the grander his position, the better for both of them. The Pig also likes the headlines, and is another first-rate bet for a Monkey businessperson. He'll work long hours quite happily while the Monkey charms the clients with expense account lunches. If the Dragon and Monkey go into advertising, the Pig and Monkey should run a mini-cab company. As for the other animals, only the Goat and Rat have anything like a chance of succeeding alongside the superior Monkey, who really is jolly clever when he wants to be, and very ambitious. The Goat will quickly learn the Monkey's stock in trade (charm and attention to detail) and might even learn enough to go it alone. If she does, she'll take the Monkey's tricks with her. The Rat is quick to sniff a bargain, and starts the bidding long before most of us are out of bed. But the Rat will want a deeper financial commitment than the Monkey is usually prepared to give, and you can't bid with one tight fist when the opposition gets tough.

On the subject of who invests what, and when, it is difficult to see how a pair of Monkeys could get along running a business. Perhaps they should forget about commerce and stick to writing comedy scripts. The Tiger's bright ideas will stimulate the Monkey, and he's intelligent enough to capitalise on them. However, he is an idealist at heart, and might easily resent the Monkey's somewhat 'personal' ethics. The honest Dog will positively reject any notion of double dealing, and the Monkey might well turn up for work one morning and find the tax inspector, VAT man and the Fraud Squad waiting on the doorstep. The Dog will have no truck with shady deals, and nor will the high-handed Rooster. When the Rooster says the cheque is in the post, she is telling the truth. The sensitive Cat should also avoid partnering a Monkey. The Cat's strength is in his methodical approach – slow but sure. But the Monkey works any odd hour, and there will again be a conflict over investment.

Not much can come from a Monkey setting up shop with a Buffalo. The Monkey uses his wits more than his muscles. And the Buffalo's attitude is far too traditional and dull for his bright and agile mind. The Snake is not crazy about working round the clock and, like the Monkey, has a wise and

Compatibility of Monkey in Business Relationships

	Bags
Rat	💰💰💰
Buffalo	
Tiger	💰💰
Cat	
Dragon	💰💰💰💰💰
Snake	💰
Horse	💰
Goat	💰💰💰
Monkey	💰💰
Rooster	
Dog	
Pig	💰💰💰💰💰

calculating head on her shoulders. Their best bet is to open up in Harley Street as a couple of high-class shrinks. They'll make an absolute fortune as long as they both have to sign cheques to withdraw cash. The Horse is practical in all matters, and both he and the Monkey like a good gossip now and again. Perhaps they should publish a society rag.

The Monkey's best partners are:
Business : Dragon
Love : Monkey
Marriage : Monkey

Monkey in Love

The Monkey usually has to face a complicated love life, full of affairs that promise more than they ever achieve. They will get away with whatever they can and will need a firm hand to bring out the best in them.

The male Dragon will easily win the heart of the lady Monkey, only it will be a bit *too* easy. The Pig is a jovial chap who likes nice soft beds and buckets of bubbly. He won't find a lady Monkey turn him down, but she must make her secret phone calls well out of earshot. Pigs don't like to be two-timed.

The Buffalo will be enchanted by the lady Monkey's bright conversation and wit. He will be put at his ease and open up his heart. 'Tell me more at my place,' says Miss Monkey. The problem is that is all the old-fashioned Buffalo will probably do. Mr Monkey will adore the lady Cat's soft skin and sensuous ways, but she will not trust the Monkey, and without it relationships do not normally last. If the Cat is uncertain as to what the Monkey tells her, the Rooster will positively disbelieve it. The trouble for the lady Rooster and the Monkey is that she sees through him after it is too late.

The Snake is wise as well as beautiful, and the male Monkey will fall for her big eyes and bewitching smile. He'll do everything he can to please her, but might find her reluctant to give him time to himself. Take care Monkey. The Tiger might easily be taken by the lady Monkey's charm, and if he falls for her he'll fall in a big way. But any affair involving two such volatile creatures is destined to be short and sweet. Nothing is forever in the lives of Monkeys and Tigers – not diamonds, not promises, and not long drawn out relationships.

The Horse knows all about vanity and it is difficult to see how a Horse and Monkey could have anything at all in common apart from self-interest. Even if two such self-centred lovers got together, what on earth would they do? The faithful and guileless Dog is in a similar fix, but for different reasons. In his case, enchanted by the Monkey's wit and charm, he'll just sit mesmerised. On the other hand, the pleasure-seeking Goat can easily handle the Monkey's tricks, and what's more she'll give as good as she gets. But she won't like being made a fool of. The Rat is another creature who knows how to use his charm, and the lady Monkey might well go along with him.

There will be no shortage of passion from the Rat. But will the Monkey be so open-hearted twenty-four hours a day? As for two Monkeys in love, it's a case of smiles all round. Lots of them.

Compatibility of Monkey in Love

Rat	♡♡♡♡
Buffalo	♡♡♡
Tiger	♡♡
Cat	♡♡♡
Dragon	♡♡♡♡♡
Snake	♡♡♡
Horse	
Goat	♡♡♡
Monkey	♡♡♡♡♡
Rooster	♡
Dog	
Pig	♡♡♡♡♡

Elizabeth Taylor
(*Rex Features Ltd*)

Shirley Conran
(*Rex Features Ltd*)

Koo Stark
(*Rex Features Ltd*)

Pope John Paul II
(*Rex Features Ltd*)

Tim Rice
(*Popperfoto*)

Duchess of Windsor
(*Rex Features Ltd*)

Diana Ross
(*Rex Features Ltd*)

Sebastian Coe
(*City Syndication Ltd*)

Monkey in Marriage

Two Monkeys; the perfect match. Wise, sociable and witty, they complement each other in every respect. And their little tricks cancel each other out.

Whereas the faithful Dog is no lover for the Monkey, he is a good bet as a husband. He will protect the Monkey from extremes and in return, she'll help him to laugh at himself. But the Monkey must be careful when laughing at her Buffalo hubby. He might think she is ridiculing him. The Monkey might easily marry a Cat, who is amused in the way only Cats can be by his wit. But Monkeys adore to travel, and Cats love their homes. A red light here, I'm afraid.

Mr Monkey will make the Tigress feel responsible as a result of his odd hours and even odder tricks. But it is an adopted role, and she'll grow resentful of it. The Snake and Monkey can make a match. Both are wise over money, but both cannot help wanting to possess what they love. More giving needed here to make it last.

Rats are generous and passionate. The best pairing is a Monkey man and a lady Rat. Both know a good thing when it comes along, but they must make certain the good thing is not another Rat or Monkey. The Goat makes no bones about what she wants from marriage – a big family and plenty of fun. Monkeys also like to enjoy themselves, and their families. Nothing will go wrong so long as the Goat and Monkey have fun *together* occasionally.

The lady Rooster's idea of fun, though, is a spending spree and the Monkey won't approve. The latest creation from Paris is not a sound investment for the Monkey's carefully invested income. However, money won't be the bone of contention should the Monkey ever marry the Horse. It will be a case of vanity splitting them up. No wedding bells here. But ding-dong for the Pig. She'll provide the home, and when times are bad, her goodwill and self-esteem will help them both. Chimes from the steeple for the Dragon, too. He will be utterly enchanted by his Monkey wife, who will do everything she possibly can to keep his powerful gaze centred on her. And she'll never be short of compliments (how cleverly she engineers them). Roll on the Golden Wedding celebrations.

Compatibility with Monkey in Marriage

Rat	🐵🐵🐵
Buffalo	🐵🐵
Tiger	🐵🐵
Cat	🐵🐵
Dragon	🐵🐵🐵🐵🐵
Snake	🐵🐵🐵
Horse	□
Goat	🐵🐵🐵🐵
Monkey	🐵🐵🐵🐵🐵
Rooster	□
Dog	🐵🐵🐵
Pig	🐵🐵🐵🐵🐵

How you will be influenced in the Year of the Monkey

A Year for Fun and Fantasy

A five-star year for the Monkey, and apart from the resolute and responsible Buffalo, who cannot take the Monkey's games at any price, it's by and large a better than average year all round. The Rooster, though, shares the Buffalo's high principles and is also deeply conservative. The only way for the Rooster to make anything of the Monkey's year is to keep away from arguments and her nose to the grindstone. The honest and loyal Dog gets tricked into the idea that he can play the same game as everyone else, but after a promising start is quickly disillusioned. It's all too fanciful. Sensitive and refined, the Cat will nevertheless give the more outrageous schemes a try. But where is the method to it all? The truth is there isn't one. And the question the rebellious Tiger will ask is, 'What on earth am I rebelling against?'

Although not a disastrous year for the Cat or the Tiger – far from it – both will end up joining the Dog in wondering why it all went wrong? A much better year for the Rat, however, who faced lean times during the previous twelve months. He'll quickly latch onto the Monkey's mood and make the most of well-stocked cupboards.

There's plenty of craft and cunning in the air, lucky Rat. The wise Snake likes to move thoughtfully and feel her way carefully – the Monkey swings high in the trees. If the Snake doesn't try to play the Monkey at his own game, she will end up with a reasonably healthy bank account. But it won't be easy money. The independent Horse must also take life as he finds it, and use his practical skills in making sure he isn't duped over financial deals. Not a good year for Horses to marry, or fall in love. On the other hand, Goats would do well to marry in a Monkey's year. But they must not invest or spend a single penny more than they have to.

The boastful, parading Dragon will shine as always, but the carnival leader must remember that he has already had his year, and the Monkey enjoys an audience. The Dragon might well find himself the butt of a few jokes, but he'll be consoled by the wage increase and the price he paid for his new car. The honest and hard-working Pig will find life plain sailing, and whatever he touches will turn if not to gold, at least to something almost as valuable. And it is also a splendid year for Pigs in love. As for the Monkey himself, it will be smiles all round, from the bank manager to the magistrate. It would be hard to find a bigger success story than a Monkey in a Monkey's year.

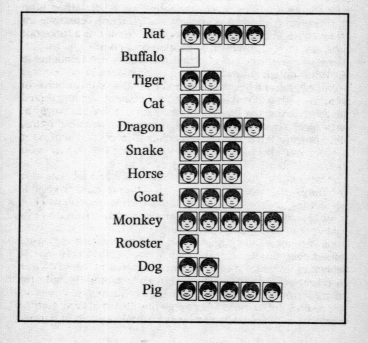

Famous Monkeys

Sebastian Coe

No matter what profession they choose, a Monkey will always depend on his great intellectual skills. The sciences are what Monkeys excel in and when a Monkey becomes a world class athlete, they will have certainly done so with more than a little help from the stuff up top; the appliance of science. Sebastian Coe is a Monkey.

Seb Coe was born in Sheffield on September 29, 1956. No other athlete has been more successful in exploiting the sport's scientific possibilities, even though it was his father who first saw how such an approach would greatly enhance an athlete's performance. Pundits say that Peter Coe's influence has been profound, which is true up to a point.

But viewed from the Chinese Horoscope, the relationship between Seb and his father is quite the reverse. Peter Coe was born in the year of the Goat, and Goats need to be tethered to make the most of their lives. In this respect, Peter tethered himself to his gifted son, and in so doing created the platform on which Seb was to build his success. In business terms, Monkeys and Goats have a better chance than most of making a partnership bear fruit – three out of a possible five stars on the compatibility chart.

Even today, with his best running years behind him, Seb Coe continues to find his father's shadow looming large. But whatever Peter Coe's sway, and as trainer he holds plenty, it is the Monkey whose influence dominates Sebastian Coe's life. And it does so off the track as well as on.

On the track, Seb Coe's running achievements are truly remarkable. During just forty-one days in 1977 the young Sebastian emerged from relative obscurity to smash three world records; the 800 metres, 1,500 metres and the mile. No one had ever held all three records simultaneously. It was an astonishing feat created from a brilliantly conceived tactical scheme drawn from a lifetime's preparation. No other runner had given so much consideration to training. Whereas his rivals have always placed great emphasis on road work and running distances, Seb Coe's more scientific approach has centred around low mileage. Wisely, he enlisted a group of university experts in medicine physiology to help construct his training programme. Consultants on bio mechanics were called in to show how Coe could concentrate on each muscle individually with the new and highly technological gym equipment that is now available. As a result of all this brain inspired muscle development, Seb Coe runs like no other athlete. Like a Monkey gliding through the trees, Seb Coe's style is effortless; so perfect, in fact, that the heels of his running shoes are virtually untouched.

Off the track, there is yet more evidence of the Monkey influence. Monkeys can't help mimicking. Pull a face and a Monkey will pull one right back. Seb Coe is a gifted impressionist and a character whose voice he has perfected is Arthur, the character in the TV series, *Minder.* The George Cole character is something of a hero to Seb, and again, he imitates Arthur's wheeler-dealer nature (which is also a strong Monkey characteristic). Coe once bought a batch of poor quality cassette players and flogged them off to his mates. And it must be said that Monkeys are careful with what they earn. They are commonly thought by the Chinese to be a bit tight-fisted. Seb was once given a Ford Granada free by Hertz, but he changed it for a smaller car because it was too heavy on petrol. And he hounded his poor sister for an outstanding £150 that she owed on a holiday she booked through his travel and leisure company. But money will never be a problem for Seb. He is already hugely rich, picking up a cool £10,000 a year from the Sport's Council for a two-and-a-half day week.

Entering his third decade, the Monkey Coe is always the realist. With a degree in economics and social history, and the inevitable decline of his physical powers, Seb sums up his future with typical Monkey acumen: 'Running's important to me. I don't ever want to be seen running badly. Even when I lose I want to feel I have lost well. I like to feel I have always given value for money, and by the time I would be an anonymous part of any race I hope I would be long out of it.' Wise Monkey.

Elizabeth Taylor and Richard Burton (Buffalo)

There are some animal signs who never give up. No matter what, Rats, Snakes and Dogs will cling like hell when asked to. But sticking to their last is not the Monkey's style; tenacity is not one of their qualities. Monkeys are far too practical. When a course of action seems doomed, the Monkey is quick to spot it and packs his bags. And there'll be no tears. There is more than just a little of the fast quitting Monkey influence at work in Liz Taylor – especially when it comes to wedding bells.

Elizabeth Taylor was born in England of American parents on February 27, 1932. Her ability to pull out when the going looks rough makes impressive reading. In 1950, she married playboy Nicky Hilton. It lasted a few months. Two years later she walked down the aisle again. This time with Michael Wilding. Born in the year of the Rat, Wilding and Liz managed to stay together four years, which is par for the course – Monkeys and Rats get a three to five star rating for compatibility. Miss Taylor's next hubby was a Goat, the film giant, Mike Todd. Again, three stars. How long their marriage would have lasted can only be guessed at since Todd was killed in an air crash in 1958. Ever resourceful, Liz then married a five star partner – a Dragon. Crooner Eddie Fisher and his bride created the Hollywood scandal of the decade. It too failed.

In between marriages, Liz Taylor twice found herself close to death. She nearly died giving birth to her daughter, Liza. In 1961 she struggled back from the brink following an acute case of pneumonia. But Monkeys have a wonderful ability to recover, stemming from their great reserves of mental stamina. Yet if Monkeys sense when a good thing's over, they find it almost impossible to let go of something they *really* want. And they usually get their tail bitten in the process. Richard Burton bit Liz Taylor's tail. And a lot more.

The son of a coal miner, Richard Burton was born in the Year of the Buffalo, on October 10, 1925. No one figure illustrates with more clarity the introvert Buffalo male. No one demonstrates their complexity of spirit with greater clarity. At one end, the Buffalo is capable of sublime greatness. At the other they can wreck the lives of anyone who breaks through their tightly controlled defences. Mostly, though, they wreck themselves. In matters of love they are hopeless. The same day Richard Burton married his first wife Sybil he went to bed with someone else. A heavy drinker, womaniser and spendthrift, Burton was fired by a worthless ambition. Worthless because it can never be proven. He said often: 'I want to be the richest, most famous actor in the world.' Had he wanted to have been the *best* actor, his ambition would have been realised.

Buffaloes and Monkeys have a fifty/fifty chance of making marriage work, and no one would deny that Liz Taylor certainly played her part in keeping the boat afloat. But after marrying and divorcing twice, even the adaptable and agile minded Monkey found she had no tricks left up her sleeve. The Buffalo was raging out of control. Burton's way of showing his love was to give jewellery. By the time it was finally over, Burton had given Liz jewels worth over £4 million. Contrast that with the single red rose she sent to his funeral and you have some idea of the gulf between their levels of emotional understanding.

However, a powerful chemistry existed between Liz and Richard Burton. It grew, I am certain, from the depth of their animal influences. Both signs have produced individuals of extraordinary greatness and though they may achieve their goals along quite different routes, there is no shortage of mutual understanding. From understanding there can grow deep love.

With Burton now dead – 'I smoked too much, drank too much and made love too much' – Liz continues her Monkey tricks. But like all Monkey women, she is a perfect mother, putting her children's welfare above all other considerations. And in spite of the Monkey's low moral horizons, she has at least married most of the men she has had affairs with. But being a Monkey, I'll leave her with the last word (they deem it their right). 'I know I'm vulgar,' she once said, 'but would you have me any other way?'

Leonardo da Vinci

Ask anyone to name just one great painting and the chances are, after a moment's head scratching, that they will answer, the *Mona Lisa*. It may, in fact, be the only painting they know. If pushed, you might also get the name of the artist from your instant art buff. And it is not inappropriate that the world's most acclaimed work of art should have been painted by a Monkey. Monkeys love to play tricks, and there can be little doubt that the *Mona Lisa*'s popularity has everything to do with a kind of trick, for that is what her enigmatic smile must surely be. Nowhere in art is there anything like it.

Leonardo da Vinci was born, as his name suggests, in Vinci, in Italy during the Monkey year; on April 15, 1452. Leonardo was the illegitimate son of a Florentine bigwig and began to display his gifts early. It is recorded that his tutor more or less gave up painting after seeing one particular canvas his brilliant young student had completed.

Monkeys like to keep their agile fingers in many pies, and Leonardo was no exception. During his life –he died in 1519, aged sixty-seven, Leonardo turned his hand to many branches of the arts. With the Monkey's adaptability clearly demonstrating itself in great depth, Leonardo went from strength to strength. And Monkeys have a vain streak which prevents them from keeping their skills hidden under wraps. Typically, Leonardo was not slow to realise his talents, nor tardy in bringing them to the attention of others. When looking for a patron, Leonardo wrote to the Duke of Milan. He ended his letter with these words: 'I can give you complete satisfaction as anyone in the construction of buildings, both public and private . . . I can further execute sculpture in marble, bronze or clay, and in painting I can do as much as anyone, whoever he may be.' He got the job.

The Chinese claim that those born in a Monkey year have a remarkable thirst for knowledge which leads them to possess a unique mind. A Monkey's grey matter is a bit like the rag and bone man's cart, full of a variety of bits and pieces which are then recycled as something else. Because they are nature's number one investigators, they must try everything – at least once. They are inquisitive and acquisitive in equal proportions. Leonardo was all these things. As well as being the first anatomist, he more or less discovered the circulation of the blood. He invented the forerunner of the tank and drew plans for the first flying machines (including the helicopter) and anticipated the submarine by some five hundred years. And all this was achieved outside his profession as a painter and sculptor. Monkeys, remember, are born under the sign of fantasy.

Monkeys are extremely practical and when a project looks like failing, they seldom cling to the hope it will turn out all right in the end. At one stage in his career, Leonardo decided he would paint a mural using an antique method which employed wax as one of the main ingredients. It was a disaster, and after three fruitless years, Leonardo simply abandoned his wall, unfinished. When a Monkey leaps from one branch to another, should one not take his weight, the Monkey quickly grabs one that will. They don't hang around.

On his death, Leonardo left thousands of pages of notes. They covered his whole range of interests and ran into millions of words. Their content astounds us even today, so rich are they in their observations, investigations and intellectual consistency. What is more, the artful Monkey's hand is apparent in every line, for Leonardo da Vinci wrote his extraordinary collection of notes back to front. To read them, you must hold his notes to a mirror!

Shirley Conran

Of the twelve animal signs that make up the Chinese Horoscopes, there is no animal more adaptable then the Monkey. Add to this the fact that they are quick witted, sharp in their business dealings and never slow to spot an opportunity, and you have an animal sign that has few rivals in commerce. Capable of using every trick in the book, the Monkey is bound to succeed. The Chinese go so far as to say that the Monkey can get one over every other animal, with the exception of the Dragon. But even the Dragon might find his fire gets a little damp unless he keeps his wits about him. And the sign does not favour either male or female Monkeys. Both can make it if they only half try. Shirley Conran is a perfect example of the female Monkey.

Born on September 21, 1922, Shirley Conran had a head start in the race to be successful. She went to both private and finishing schools before a period at art school, where she studied sculpture. She was twenty-three when she married Terence Conran. The marriage produced two talented children, Jasper and Sebastian, but little else. It ended in tatters after eight years. Terence Conran is a Goat, and Monkeys and Goats have a better than even chance of making a go of marriage, a point that is proved by Shirley and Terry trying it a second time. But it didn't work out. However, Goats and Monkeys do have plenty in common, especially in business. Terry and Shirley clearly influenced each other at the beginning, and there's no doubt that they were profoundly aware of Britain's awakening to the liberated woman and their views on the home. Shirley Conran was the first home editor of the *Daily Mail* and first Woman's Page editor of *The Observer Colour Magazine.* These two jobs were enormously influential and required buckets of the Monkey's great organisational skills.

Although she was well respected as an editor, Shirley Conran only became really big news following the runaway success of her first novel. *Lace* was a blockbuster and relied considerably on explicit sex scenes to sell it. Once again, Shirley's animal sign came in handy as Monkeys know all there is to know about sex. The Chinese say that the Monkey does not have a very moral view of the world, and bends morality to fit his own needs. They also say that Monkeys adore sexual intrigue, often more than the act itself. But anyone can write a book about sex, and as Shirley herself put it: 'Anyone can write. The trick is getting other people to read it.'

Monkeys are universally known, feared, and respected for their bag of tricks. Shirley Conran's novels are typical of the tricky Monkey in that they are not all her own work. What she cannot do herself, Shirley gets others to do for her. And you won't always find a Monkey quick to give the credit to those who deserve it. One of Shirley's co-authors once arrived to find the door locked and her manuscript inside. But Shirley dismisses her co-author's claims with a typical Monkey quip: 'I'm thinking of hiring the Albert Hall,' she was reported to have said, 'for a reunion of all the women who say they write my books.'

Whatever the extent of her co-author's contribution to the rise of Shirley Conran the novelist, few would deny her skill for knowing what the public want and giving it to them. Today, she lives in Monte Carlo, London, *and* owns a castle in France. Some call her ruthless, but that isn't a Monkey quality. Crafty, yes; tricky, yes. But not ruthless. And there's no shortage of wisdom. As Shirley Conran points out: 'Life is too short to stuff a mushroom.' We know what she means.

Monkeys have a rather high opinion of themselves, and they are often superficial in their judgement of others

Famous Monkeys

Media/Entertainment

Francesca Annis
Michael Aspel
Bobby Ball
Carol Barnes
Hywell Bennett
Lionel Blair
Frank Bough
Faith Brown
Dave Brubeck
Yul Brynner
Ian Carmichael
Johnny Cash
Roy Castle
Shirley Conran
Alistair Cooke
Ray Davies
Bette Davis
Jonathan Dimbleby
Percy Edwards
Andrew Gardner
Greer Garson
Sam Goldwyn
Dulcie Gray
Arthur Hailey
Rex Harrison
Fred Housego
Jane Lapotaire
Bob Marley
Robert Morley
Peter O'Toole
Beryl Reid
Tim Rice
Angela Rippon
Diana Ross
Omar Sharif
Martin Shaw
James Stewart
Rod Stewart
Liz Taylor

Sport

Bjorn Borg
Donald Bradman
Sebastian Coe
Tony Jacklin
Charlie Magri
Brian Moore
Ray Reardon
Sugar Ray Robinson
Tessa Sanderson
Alex Stepney

Arts (Literature, Music)

Ray Bradbury
Cartier Bresson
Lord Byron
Charles Dickens
Godfrey Evans
F. Scott Fitzgerald
Ian Fleming
Antonia Fraser
Paul Gauguin
W. S. Gilbert
W. G. Grace
Osbert Lancaster
Modigliani
Ronald Searle

Johnny Speight
Koo Stark
Isaac Stern
Leonardo da Vinci
Christopher Wren

Politics
Joseph Chamberlain
Roy Hattersley
Garfield Todd

Marcia Williams

Others
Buddha
Malcolm Campbell
Descartes
Harry Houdini
Pope John Paul II
Duchess of Windsor

A Special Word on Compatibility

Throughout this book I have done my best to translate the Chinese view of compatibility with that of our own. But there are distinct differences between our two cultures which need clarification.

For the Chinese, love is seldom seen as something separate from marriage, an experience to be enjoyed in isolation. It is seen as part of a natural progression. In other words, love and marriage are thought of as a whole, and in this context their system of grading the compatibility of animal signs makes a lot of sense. In the West, if we have a love affair, we do so aware that it might or might not work out. In China that is not the case; there a couple find love later, accepting marriage as a kind of business relationship which is impossible to dissolve, no matter what. In China, it is imperative, therefore, that a Dragon, say, should marry a Rat, Rooster or Monkey; a Horse should marry a Goat, and a Dog should marry a Tiger.

But whatever your choice, the compatibility charts should not be read like the Ten Commandments, and not taken as law. They are more akin to a 'Good Food Guide'. We often enjoy meals in places with no stars, and are disappointed by five-star restaurants. It is the same with compatibility. If your partner is zero rated, but you love them, that's fine.

What the charts do, however, is prepare you for the future. Few people know what to expect when they embark on a new relationship. The changes that take place when a relationship develops badly are those we have all experienced; a sense of surprise followed by a sense of frustration. 'If only I had known this or that about him, or her', is a more than familiar expression, one we have almost certainly used ourselves. Quite simply, the job of the compatibility charts is to take the sting out of such a process. To be warned is to be prepared.

Above all, the compatibility charts provide a choice, saying if you want a relationship that is tailor made then here are the candidates. And if you want to put your money on an outsider, then it's up to you. But in any event, it must be emphasised that the compatibility charts are not carved in stone. At the same time, it is also worth remembering that they have been in existence for thousands of years. That they have stood the test of time, is, I believe, a tribute to their effectiveness.

Famous Monkey Pairs, Couples and Groups

Elizabeth Taylor and Richard Burton   (Buffalo)
Mrs Simpson and the Duke of Windsor   (Horse)
Tim Rice and Andrew Lloyd Webber   (Rat)
Diana Ross and Mary Wilson   (both Monkeys)

Find Your Partner's and Friends' Animal Signs

The Rat

1900	January 31st to February 18th	1901
1912	February 18th to February 5th	1913
1924	February 5th to January 23rd	1925
1936	January 24th to February 10th	1937
1948	February 10th to January 28th	1949
1960	January 28th to February 14th	1961
1972	January 15th to February 2nd	1973
1984	February 2nd to February 19th	1985

The Buffalo

1901	February 19th to February 7th	1902
1913	February 6th to January 25th	1914
1925	January 24th to February 12th	1926
1937	February 11th to January 30th	1938
1949	January 29th to February 16th	1950
1961	February 15th to February 4th	1962
1973	February 3rd to January 22nd	1974
1985	February 20th to February 8th	1986

The Tiger

1902	February 8th	to	January 28th	1903
1914	January 26th	to	February 13th	1915
1926	February 13th	to	February 1st	1927
1938	January 31st	to	February 18th	1939
1950	February 17th	to	February 5th	1951
1962	February 5th	to	January 24th	1963
1974	January 23rd	to	February 10th	1975
1986	February 9th	to	January 28th	1987

The Cat

1903	January 29th	to	February 15th	1904
1915	February 14th	to	February 2nd	1916
1927	February 2nd	to	January 22nd	1928
1939	February 19th	to	February 7th	1940
1951	February 6th	to	January 26th	1952
1963	January 25th	to	February 12th	1964
1975	February 11th	to	January 30th	1976
1987	January 29th	to	February 16th	1988

The Dragon

1904	February 16th to February 3rd	1905
1916	February 3rd to January 22nd	1917
1928	January 23rd to February 9th	1929
1940	February 8th to January 26th	1941
1952	January 27th to February 13th	1953
1964	February 13th to February 1st	1965
1976	January 31st to February 17th	1977
1988	February 17th to February 5th	1989

The Snake

1905	February 4th to January 24th	1906
1917	January 23rd to February 10th	1918
1929	February 10th to January 29th	1930
1941	January 27th to February 14th	1942
1953	February 14th to February 2nd	1954
1965	February 2nd to January 20th	1966
1977	February 18th to February 6th	1978
1989	February 6th to January 26th	1990

The Horse

1906	January 25th to February 12th	1907
1918	February 11th to January 31st	1919
1930	January 30th to February 16th	1931
1942	February 15th to February 4th	1943
1954	February 3rd to January 23rd	1955
1966	January 21st to February 8th	1967
1978	February 7th to January 27th	1979

The Goat

1907	February 13th to February 1st	1908
1919	February 1st to February 19th	1920
1931	February 17th to February 5th	1932
1943	February 5th to January 24th	1944
1955	January 24th to February 11th	1956
1967	February 9th to January 29th	1968
1979	January 28th to February 15th	1980

The Rooster

1909	January 22nd to February 9th	**1910**
1921	February 8th to January 27th	**1922**
1933	January 26th to February 13th	**1934**
1945	February 13th to February 1st	**1946**
1957	January 31st to February 17th	**1958**
1969	February 17th to February 5th	**1970**
1981	February 5th to January 24th	**1982**

The Dog

1910	February 10th to January 29th	**1911**
1922	January 28th to February 15th	**1923**
1934	February 14th to February 3rd	**1935**
1946	February 2nd to January 21st	**1947**
1958	February 18th to February 7th	**1959**
1970	February 6th to January 26th	**1971**
1982	January 25th to February 12th	**1983**

The Pig

1911	January 30th	to	February 17th	1912
1923	February 16th	to	February 4th	1924
1935	February 4th	to	January 23rd	1936
1947	January 22nd	to	February 9th	1948
1959	February 8th	to	January 27th	1960
1971	January 27th	to	February 14th	1972
1983	February 13th	to	February 1st	1984

A Brief look at the other Animal Signs

The Rat
The Rat is born under the sign of charm. Rats are warm, passionate and the supreme opportunist. They live for the day and seldom plan for tomorrow. Time does not concern them. Rats have sharp wits and an eye for detail, which favours them if they choose to become writers. Rats make excellent critics and salesmen. However, Rats have an undercurrent of aggression which occasionally expresses itself in worrying over details. In extreme cases, some Rats undergo a complete reversal and become obsessed by making plans and keeping statistics. Such Rats should not be rubbed up the wrong way. All Rats are devoted and love their family. They care little about their surroundings and are uncomplicated in affairs of the heart. Rats make money, but they cannot hold on to it. Rats love to scheme. They have a tendency to grumble when things go wrong.

The Buffalo
The Buffalo is born under the twin signs of equilibrium and tenacity. Buffalo people are conservative with a big and small

C, even if they hide behind a façade of being Left Wing. They work exceptionally hard and are strong and resolute in their business dealings. As parents they are firm and authoritative. Buffaloes are great achievers and feature prominently on the World Stage. They do not suffer fools, but find self criticism difficult. Buffaloes are stubborn and reliable, but they have complex hearts. In matters of romance they are often all at sea, seldom building lasting relationships. When a Buffalo has a conviction, he makes it the centrepiece of his life. Without conviction, a Buffalo can easily go to seed. Buffaloes do not care to share power. They love tradition and gardening.

The Tiger

Tigers are born under the sign of courage. They are brave, powerful people with a strong sense of their personal identity. They are natural revolutionaries and are disrespectful of authority. Tigers are quick tempered, and will risk everything for any cause that they believe in. This is particularly true of a Tiger in love. Tigers are great on ideas, seeming to possess a never-ending stream of original schemes. But the Tiger is a short paced creature and after a fast start, they are likely to run out of breath. They love to be the boss figure, usually ending up in charge of a team. The Tiger's life is often full of danger, and Tigers live life to the full. This sometimes means that a Tiger will meet a tragic and sudden end. Most of all, a Tiger needs to become fully himself, no matter what the cost. In other words, a Tiger needs to show the world what they are made of. They are very generous.

The Cat

Cats are born under the sign of virtue. They are social and refined with a good nose for bargains. Cats have good manners, good taste and place a high premium on family life. They are methodical, sometimes obsessively so. Cats are extremely diplomatic and are good listeners. Not original, Cats nevertheless show a great appreciation of beauty. They have shrewd artistic judgement and are acquisitive. Once a Cat has struck a deal he will keep it, come what may. Some Cats become ruthless when given power beyond their capability, but they are not normally concerned with matters outside domestic life. Cats hate change in routine and are sometimes a bit snobbish. Cats respond poorly to pressure, and will cave in emotionally under stress. A Cat's advice is well intentioned. They take their time when coming to a decision, and are very sensuous. All Cats dress well.

The Dragon

Dragons are born under the sign of luck. They are the national symbol of China and are believed to bring the three great eastern benedictions: wealth, long life and harmony. Dragons often become national heroes and have a magnetic personality. They are loved by many, but seldom love deeply in return. Dragons are impulsive, hot-headed and strive relentlessly for perfection. They have big hearts, broad interests and their advice is very wise. Dragons offer both their wisdom and professions of love freely and often. Dragons are generous, but often let their hearts rule their heads. Once they have begun a task, they see it through, regardless of its merit. Forced into a corner, the Dragon makes a poor judge and an even worse diplomat. They hate routine. Full of self-confidence, the Dragon can achieve anything.

The Snake
Snakes are born under the sign of wisdom. Guided by intuition, Snakes are wise, intelligent and think deeply. Snakes have a restless intellect which causes them to change direction many times in life. Although they do not give up easily, Snakes go through long periods of inactivity. This usually happens before a major change. Snakes are poor gamblers, and when asked to decide quickly, often make the wrong decision. They are possessive in human relationships and cling to those they love. Snakes are both peaceful and artistic, and have the gifts of music and humour. They are also capable of great artistic innovation. Snake women have the power to bewitch. Unlucky in love, Snakes can make a lot of money when they need to, and can become extremely wealthy. Snakes don't give up.

The Horse
The Horse is born under the twin signs of elegance and ardour. Horses are industrious and display a marked independence in everything they do. All Horses have great personality, which they trade on. They take naturally to any job that gives them freedom and a chance to exercise their great stamina. However, Horses become quickly bored and constantly take up

new interests. When in love, the Horse becomes weak and unsure of himself. To make matters worse, Horses fall in love very easily. Although normally even tempered, the Horse can be provoked to terrible rages. Something of an egoist, the Horse can lead any crowd. He does not suffer fools and seldom gives an opinion without careful consideration. Horse women are witty and sociable.

The Goat

The Goat is born under the sign of art, and as their sign suggests love all things beautiful. Goats are society's peace-makers and adore good company. They love the *dolce vita* and are usually acquisitive. Goats pay a lot of attention to their homes and maintain strong family ties. They have, however, a capricious side to their nature which expresses itself most notably in a fickle heart. Goats are fine hosts and generous to their friends. Although they excel in all branches of the arts, they do not make good businessmen. Goats often overstate their case, or chose the wrong moment to make a point. Goats do better when not left to initiate the first move. Once tethered, so to speak, Goats may become extremely successful. A Goat's views are often superficial, influenced by trend. Thoughtful and amusing, the Goat's main problem is coming to terms with his natural waywardness.

The Rooster

The Rooster is born under the sign of candour. They speak their minds frankly and openly, and always truthfully. They are deeply conservative, orderly in their daily lives, but have a boastful manner. Never short of an opinion, Roosters are sociable and spend much of their time dreaming up schemes which seldom bear fruit. In matters of finance, Roosters are either thrifty or spendthrifts; nothing in between. They are keen gardeners and adore home life. Successful in business, Roosters love the limelight, but they lack initiative and are best in partnership. Although they like to dress up and put on a show, Roosters are old fashioned in affairs of the heart. Roosters are honest, talkative and incorruptible. They regard their love life as strictly private and hold moral views on all matters. Roosters born between the hours of 5 and 7 are the most vocal. Lacking tact, Roosters are models of generosity. All Roosters are methodical.

The Dog

Dogs are born under the sign of loyalty. All Dogs are faithful, with warm hearts and a touchingly honest approach to everything they do. Dogs frequently find themselves defending those less fortunate and are just in their judgements. They fight bravely when roused, but have a tendency to act stubbornly. Dogs are practical in business but dither in the face of romance. Once set a worthwhile task, a Dog will never give up. They are watchful and often argumentative. The Dog's big problem is his constant anxiety. All Dogs suffer from an inability to stop worrying over details. They are occasionally blunt in their public dealings, but are easy going and delightful when in the company of friends. Dogs are good to their parents and never hypocritical. If he can tell the wood from the trees, a Dog will be a success. Dogs who have suffered bad experiences should be avoided. Dog women are often very vivacious.

The Pig

The Pig is born under the sign of honesty. Pigs are hard working and fun loving. Pigs enjoy all forms of social life and throw themselves into both work and leisure with great gusto. Big hearted, Pigs are jovial and forthright. They are lucky in business and seem to be able to make money whenever they want. In the matters of romance, Pigs are straightforward and direct; they are not ones for sophisticated courtship. Well informed and robust in character, the Pig is dependable and organises his life to suit himself. Sometimes the Pig has too high an opinion of his worth. Here he can be duped in his financial affairs or jilted in romance. Pigs adore their family and are generous with invitations to their homes. Slow to anger, Pigs are sometimes too gossipy for their own good. Men Pigs are often fancy dressers. Pigs are best in partnerships.

Author's Note

The Year of the Cat

Is it the year of the Cat, Rabbit or Hare? On the surface it is all a bit confusing, but there is a very simple explanation. The name you adopt depends very largely on which part of the world you come from. This is how it works.

Although it is true to say that the Chinese invented their wonderful horoscope, they are not the only ones who use it. During the 2,000 years it has been in existence the Chinese Horoscope has now travelled around the world. But if the horoscopes are new to us in the West, they have been with the nations close to China since the very start – well, almost. Not unnaturally each new country refined the twelve animal signs of the horoscope to suit themselves, to fit in with their particular culture. For instance, the people of Hong Kong name what the Chinese call the Rabbit, the Hare. In Vietnam, Cambodia and Korea, the Rabbit is called the Cat. The reason is simple. These people consider the word 'Rabbit' an insult. Likewise, many Chinese are offended at being termed a Cat.

My own researches show that the very first written word for the Cat/Rabbit/Hare year was, in Chinese, a 'creature with soft fur and a weak back'. Clearly it is a description which can easily fit all three animals.

Curiously the West did not learn about the Chinese Horoscopes from the Chinese, but from the Vietnamese who settled in France following the Indochinese war in the 50s. This is why so many Westerners call the years 1903, 1915, 1927, 1939, 1951, 1963, 1975 and 1987 the Year of the Cat.

But the most important point of all is to remember that all the experts agree that no matter what the word – Cat, Rabbit or Hare, the influence is *exactly the same!*

Also, the Rooster is sometimes called the Cock, the Buffalo the Ox, the Goat the Sheep and the Pig the Boar.

The author is grateful to the following reference sources for additional material:

Chinese Horoscopes by Paula Delsol, (Pan)
The Way to Chinese Astrology: the Four Pillars of Wisdom Jean-Michel Huon de Kermadec, (Unwin)
The Handbook of Chinese Horoscopes Theodora Lau, (Arrow).